I Can Feel Blue on Monday

Marc Maurer
Editor

Large Type Edition

A KERNEL BOOK
published by
NATIONAL FEDERATION OF THE BLIND

TABLE OF CONTENTS

Marc Maurer, President
National Federation of the Blind

Editor's Introduction

The year 2000 marks the sixtieth anniversary of the National Federation of the Blind. In the six decades of our existence we have worked with energy to make lives better for blind people. Our projects have been many and varied, and we have had much help from our sighted friends. In the early days few of us had jobs of any kind, and the outlook was often bleak.

Today much has changed. Many of us have jobs and families and hopes and dreams. There are problems still, but the future is bright with promise.

I believe that the progress we are making is due in no small part to the growing understanding of our tens of thousands of regular Kernel Book readers. The present volume, *I Can Feel Blue on Monday*, is number nineteen in the series.

Here you will meet old friends and new—the real blind men and women whose stories tell what blindness is and, perhaps equally important, what it is not.

Although our problems often seem complex, they frequently result from simple matters of misunderstanding and lack of information. How does a little boy who is blind deal with his teacher who insists that he could feel colors if only he would try a little harder? How does a blind tourist absorb the splendor of the palace of the Imperial Chinese Emperor? What about the woman with failing eyesight who can no longer see the beautiful wings of a butterfly—can she no longer hope to experience those magical moments of beauty which once moved her to tears? And, finally, if (as Thomas Edison once said) 80 percent of all we learn comes through the eye, can our hope for normal lives be anything more than a futile dream?

You who are readers of previous Kernel Books already know our answer to that last question, and you who are new to the series will learn now that it is a resounding "No!" For in these pages—the record of our triumphs and tribulations, our hopes and fears, our failures and accomplishments—is told the story of our struggle to achieve the things that give life joy and purpose.

Meaningful work, a chance to be of service to our fellow human beings, families bound together in love—these are the things we want for ourselves and those who will come after us. You understand these things. After all, they are what you want, too— which brings me to the central message of this Kernel Book and the eighteen which have preceded it. I've said it before, and I'll no doubt say it again: We who are blind are pretty much like you. We are, that is, if we have the chance to try. We have our share of both geniuses and jerks, but most of us are somewhere between—ordinary people living regular lives.

We are looking for understanding and friendship. We are looking for colleagues like you. We believe that we can help to build a better world, and this belief comes, at least in part, from the response we have had from the Kernel Books.

Marc Maurer
Baltimore, Maryland
2000

WHY LARGE TYPE?

The type size used in this book is 14 point for two important reasons: One, because typesetting of 14 point or larger complies with federal standards for the printing of materials for visually impaired readers, and we want to show you what type size is helpful for people with limited sight.

The second reason is that many of our friends and supporters have asked us to print our paperback books in 14-point type so they too can easily read them. Many people with limited sight do not use Braille. We hope that by printing this book in a larger type than customary, many more people will be able to benefit from it.

*A seven-year-old Marc Maurer relaxes
in the back yard.*

No Light from Thomas Edison

by Marc Maurer

There is a persistently repeated rumor that the vast majority of all knowledge is obtained through sight—that 80 percent of all we learn comes through the eye. Since I was born blind (I had a little vision, but not much), this has been a troubling notion for me because it leaves blind people out—or almost out. The argument urges everybody to think that we who are blind have the possibility of only 20 percent of the learning that is available to everybody else. If this line of reasoning is true, blind people would win all of the contests for stupidity.

But an especially heightened level of stupidity among the blind has simply not been my experience. Sure, I have known blind people who were not so sharp, but

I've also known some who were brilliant. And most fall somewhere in between—just like the sighted people I know.

So where did this oft repeated idea that 80 percent of all knowledge is transmitted by sight come from? Several years ago I decided to try to find out.

When I traced the matter back into history, I found that it appears to be based on an advertisement created in 1923 by Thomas Edison. He had invented the film projector, and he wanted to sell it to school systems. The projector had not yet become a recognized tool of school equipment, and it was fairly expensive.

Edison needed some way to make the projector seem dramatically important. Consequently, he said that 80 percent of all learning comes through the eye. His advertisement has inadvertently created substantial problems for the blind in the decades since it first appeared.

Thomas Edison, I'm sure, didn't intend to cause all this trouble. After all, he is known for creating light. Besides, one of the announced purposes for the phonograph he invented was to record books for the blind. But this time he failed absolutely. Had he thought about it more carefully, I expect he would thoroughly have understood what we in the National Federation of the Blind have come to know about the innate normality and fundamental capacity of the blind to compete and do it successfully.

It just didn't happen to suit Mr. Edison's purposes to approach the matter from this point of view. He, after all, was trying to sell film projectors—not the capacity of blind people. Now I, on the other hand, have little interest in film projectors, but much in what is and isn't true about blindness. And, one thing I know from my own experience is that blind people learn as thoroughly as sighted people. It's just that we do it in a different way.

How we learn to do things can seem odd to people who are used to learning and doing by looking with their eyes. My own childhood is a good example.

When I was born blind my mother faced the problem of what to do with a blind child. She had no experience with blindness, and she did not know of the existence of the National Federation of the Blind. Consequently, she knew of nobody who could answer her questions. She was on her own.

My father was a travelling salesman. He was home on weekends, but rarely during the week. He had opinions aplenty about raising a blind child, but most of the time he wasn't there to help in putting them into practice.

We grew up in the Midwest. Our neighborhoods were safe, and visits from one household to another to share a plate of cookies or borrow a cup of sugar were commonplace. My brothers were permitted to roam freely anywhere within calling distance. My mother decided that the same freedom of movement should be available to me, her blind son.

I only learned later that many parents are much more restrictive. I roamed at will all over the neighborhood. I was told to stay out of the street and to stay on my own block. Otherwise, there were no restrictions. However, I was expected to come when called. Frequently, I was out of earshot when my mother called. She became annoyed with me; she told me to stay close by, but I ignored her admonitions. Finally, she decided I could not be trusted to stay close to home, and she tied me to the front porch.

Being tied to the porch didn't seem so bad to me until my mother called us for dinner. The rope was too short to let me get to the kitchen, and I thought I wouldn't be able to have anything to eat. I suspect the lesson did its trick because I was only tied to the porch once. The freedom to move and to explore also did its work as I learned to be curious—to try to discover what was on the other side of a wall or under a boulder or across the vacant lot. I suppose I was lost part of the time, but it didn't seem important. I was exploring a new place and learning about new territory. My mother told me later that she worried a lot, but she thought my exploration was more important than her worrying.

When I was about ten years old, I learned to climb ropes. My arms were not strong enough to let me do it hand over hand, so I learned to grip the rope with both feet and hands. I was fascinated with climbing, and I asked my parents to give me a piece of rope twenty-five feet long for my birthday. I wanted to hang it in a tree in our backyard.

Climbing trees had been a part of my growing-up for years, and I was certain that I could climb the one in our yard. However, twenty-five feet of rope is heavy, and I didn't know how to get a good grip on it while climbing the tree. I decided to tie one end of it around me for the climb, and what better place was there to tie it than around my neck.

With the rope secured, up the tree I went. Reaching a limb over twenty feet from the ground, I detached the rope from my neck, tied it around the limb, and slid to the ground. I had the plaything I wanted—a rope to use for a swing, to climb, and to hold a tire when I could find one. I went inside to tell my mother about it. To my surprise she seemed upset. She had looked out the window when I was about halfway up the tree. She had been faced with an awful choice: she had to decide whether she should run outside to holler at me or stay inside to let me finish my climb.

She thought that if she hollered at me I might slip. Then, I might be dangling on the end of a rope. While she was watching me go up the tree, one of our neighbors called to tell her I was in the upper branches with a rope around my neck. My mother said, "I know. I am watching him climb." It must have made the neighbors think the bunch of us were crazy. My mother asked, "Couldn't you have tied the rope around your waist?" It was a good idea. I just hadn't thought of it.

How do blind people learn? Most people possess five senses; the blind have only four—though many blind people have a small amount of remaining vision. I use these four to learn. I examine my surroundings by listening, touching, smelling, and tasting. And I try to catalog what I have discovered for comparison with previous experience.

Braille is an important mechanism for blind people to read. I learn by reading Braille, a system of raised dots arranged in different patterns for each Braille symbol. Braille can be employed to print Japanese, Chinese, mathematics, and hundreds of other languages. This is one form of learning by touch.

When I was about five years old my father gave me a beach ball. Although I was almost totally blind, I could distinguish the colors of the ball when I held it close to my face in bright sunlight. I came to know red, green, white, yellow, and blue. I have an image of these colors with me still although I have been totally blind now for thirty years.

At about the same time, I was introduced to Braille symbols. For whatever reason my mind attributed color to the characters under my fingers—not the color of the page on which the Braille was embossed, but colors independent of the paper on which they were written. For me Braille characters are green, brown, red, yellow, and black. This phenomenon seems strange even to me, but Braille symbols are to me rich with color. This makes the reading vivid in imagination.

There are those who argue that the remaining senses of a blind person—hearing, taste, smell, and touch—are heightened—that the hearing is keener and the touch more sensitive for a blind person. Some have even offered a scientific explanation. They say that the brain of a blind person is not required to do the complicated and difficult task of seeing, so it has excess capacity—which is used to provide super-computing power for the other senses. It sounds nice, but our experience suggests that it isn't so.

However, even if the blind do not hear better than the sighted, many blind people are better listeners than some sighted people are because hearing is one of the primary ways we learn.

My work with the National Federation of the Blind takes me throughout the United States, but it also sometimes requires me to visit other lands. Recently, I was invited to give a lecture at Oxford University. One of the colleges there is New College, which was established in 1379. When I asked why it was called new, officials at Oxford told me that it was new when it first came into being.

When I visit a new place, I want to know how the people in the locality live, what experiences they regard as a natural part of daily routine, what tools they use, what beliefs are fundamental to them, and what they do for fun. I want to study not only the monuments of history but also the local shops. A grocery store, a local drugstore, and a marketplace are of interest to me.

I grew up in the Midwest, a place where there is plenty of space. When I read books such as *The Three Musketeers,* I wondered how a single villainous highwayman could completely block a street, an action that seemed frequently to take place in books of high adventure. When I got to Oxford, I discovered how it was done. One of the streets there, which dated back to the time of the establishment of Oxford, was only wide enough to permit one automobile at a time to pass. A lane which led from this street to shops and pubs nearby was only four or five feet wide. One of the shops off this lane was the Turf Tavern, where they offered us such collations as Steak and Ale Pie along with Strong Bow Cider— apparently so named because when consumed in quantity it has stimulated English yeomen to engage in contests of strength. This fermented brew is said to date back to the time of Robin Hood and his band of Merry Men.

Following the trip to England, I spent two days in Paris to meet with leaders of the French Organization of the Blind. While there, I climbed as high as I could in the Eiffel Tower. I listened to the wind hundreds of feet above the ground, and I heard faint sounds from the earth far below.

Riding up in the elevator, I felt the change in air pressure, and I examined the huge girders that are a part of the structure. Later,

I held in my hands a tiny scale-model of the tower which gave me an idea of the overall shape of the structure. I could not have had as clear an understanding of the Eiffel Tower without the scaled model, but my understanding would have been equally incomplete without climbing the structure itself.

Another part of my learning involved a visit to China that I made with a Federation colleague, Mary Ellen Jernigan, to participate in meetings conducted to study programs for the blind in different parts of the world. I had never been to China before that trip, and I was curious.

I am an American, who grew to adulthood during the time of the Cold War. I had heard about communism, and I thought I might be facing hostility from those who opposed capitalism. I found the culture of China very different from what I expected and very different from any other I had experienced.

When I enter a new city or country, I begin by asking questions, but I was afraid that there might be queries which would be off limits in China. So, I approached my guides gingerly and with much courtesy. They were universally friendly, and they seemed genuinely glad that we had come to their country. Those who greeted us had arranged for a minivan to take us to our hotel. It was built by a Japanese company, and I judged that the car had seen quite a bit of use. There were homemade seat covers installed, which seemed to be quite common.

In Beijing, the capital city, there was a great deal of dust. In stores, in factories, in the public markets, in restaurants, in public places, things were often dusty. It was not that they were excessively dirty, but most things were a little dusty. It was the exception when they were sparkling clean.

When we arrived at our hotel, located in what appeared to be a light industrial center of Beijing, we were met with courtesy and an almost inexhaustible wish to serve. A chair was placed for us to use as we were being greeted and registered. Two bellmen accompanied us to our rooms along with two other officials. Shortly after we had been established in our rooms, two serving personnel came to ask us if we wanted our beds turned down for sleep. Within fifteen minutes of our arrival, six different people had asked to give us service.

In our rooms we were offered a fruit plate and a tea service with hot water and Chinese teas. The cups for the tea service were delicate, handleless, painted porcelain with porcelain covers. Often tea came to us during the trip in covered cups.

We went to Tiananmen Square the following morning, but we could not get into it. Each time we tried to cross the street to get to the square, a soldier waved us off. We learned after a time that the People's Congress was meeting in the square.

Tourists and other non-essentials were not welcome.

Mao Tse Tung proclaimed the revolution and created Red China in 1949. His name and image have meant Communist China for me for many years. We found only one picture of Mao at the entrance to the Imperial City, the Forbidden City, the Imperial Palace that is at the center of Beijing. It was a city within a city until the end of the imperial rule.

This Forbidden City was the living quarters of the Imperial Family. It consists of a number of buildings in a walled city that is a kilometer square. At the south end of the Forbidden City there are three gates. The central gate was for the emperor and empress. The left-hand gate was for the ministers of government. The right-hand gate was for everybody else. We were told that we could enter through the right-hand gate.

The lion is a symbol of imperial power, and the grounds of the palace are decorated with many pairs of lions. The male has a ball under its paw, and the lioness has a cub. A symbol of fertility is the dragon, and the palace grounds have dragons decorating the walls. We were told that over one thousand such dragons are part of the palace.

We were brought to the throne room, the empress's private quarters, the hall of China which depicts the history of the making of porcelain, the emperor's personal living chambers, and many other buildings, rooms, halls, and gardens. The impression is that the quarters for the imperial family were immense.

Some aspects of the imperial grounds were curious. There was one bedroom used by the emperor which had a space below it for a fire to be kept burning to keep the emperor warm. Many large pots of water holding hundreds of gallons were scattered throughout the palace. Several of the palace buildings were made of stone, but others were constructed of bamboo. The pots of water were kept for preventing fires. The first seismograph, it was said, originated in the Imperial Palace. The water trembling in these pots gave an indication of seismic activity. Later more sophisticated seismic equipment was developed at the palace.

One evening we were the dinner guests of the assistant director of the Chinese Braille Publishing Company. The publishing company produces both Braille and print books. The books prepared in print are sold to keep the outfit in business, and the Braille materials are distributed to about one million Braille readers in China.

The building where the publishing is done was on the outskirts of Beijing near the Marco Polo Bridge, which we were told had been built in 1192 A.D. More than five hundred lions decorate the bridge. The

Japanese invaded China in 1937, and damage from the gunfire that occurred at the time is still visible on the bridge. But, back to the dinner hosted by the China Braille Publishing Company.

We entered a restaurant in which almost nobody spoke English. The place was not heated, so I kept my overcoat. Tables in the restaurant had holes in the middle with gas fired burners in them. A pot of soup was placed on each burner. The soup was a mushroom broth. I was given a small bowl of soup—the bowl was about three inches across. When I ate this, another serving was placed in my bowl. Then several kinds of mushrooms grown in the mountains were added to the broth. When boiled, they were served into my bowl.

I ate these, and another serving came into my bowl. Soon I got the idea that if I wanted servings to stop coming, I would need to leave some of the last serving. After the mushrooms came the next course—fish balls followed by a thin spaghetti-like substance called split rice. Then we were given fish fillets, vegetables, and boiled squid. Each of the courses was boiled in the mushroom broth and served into my bowl.

The final serving was a rice ball with sesame seeds on the outside. The dinner was excellent and offered with the greatest hospitality and good humor. Though we spoke no Chinese, and our hosts spoke only rudimentary English, we had a wonderful time and became good friends.

We who are blind learn with our hands by the sense of touch, through our ears, through sound, and through our ability to smell and taste. However, mostly we learn through our ability to think and synthesize information. Seeing is one way to gather facts, but it is only one. We who do not have this faculty rely on other means to gain similar information. What we do with the knowledge is the test of whether we can compete.

Sight is valuable, and we encourage its use and preservation. However, vision does not determine the capacity to learn or the ability to think. If those with the best vision were the most intelligent, dogs would be smarter than people. As valuable as vision is, we believe that alternatives exist that will let us learn what we need to know to make contributions to our society.

We learn by climbing trees or examining the carved head of a dragon on the wall of a Chinese palace. However we do it, we want to use the knowledge we gain to bring greater independence to the blind and more opportunity to everybody. This is why we have formed the National Federation of the Blind.

Dr. Abraham Nemeth

I Can Feel Blue
on Monday

by Abraham Nemeth, Ph.D.

Some encounters blind people have with the sighted reflect serious issues of understanding. Some are humorous, others are so bizarre as to defy all reason, and still others are mixtures of all these characteristics.

Dr. Abraham Nemeth is a long-time leader in the National Federation of the Blind of Michigan and has had a distinguished career as a professor of mathematics. Here he recalls a childhood incident that brings to mind the old adage that one hardly knows whether to laugh or cry. Here is what he has to say:

I attended Evander Childs High School in the Bronx. I was the only blind student in my class. My teacher for fourth-term English was Miss Storm. On the day before the incident I am about to relate, she had given us a lecture about free association and how this could stimulate the imagination.

On this eventful afternoon she distributed a sheet of special paper to each student. "Now I want you to use this sheet of paper as the basis of free association," she said. "I want you to smell it, tear it, rumple it, take note of its color, and, on the basis of the impressions that come to you, I want you to write a composition of about 150 words."

When she had finished distributing the sheets of paper to the other students she stopped at my seat with a sheet of this magic paper. I dutifully smelled it, tore it, crumpled it, following all the instructions. Finally she asked: "What color is it?" "I don't know," I said. "I can't see color."

"Helen Keller can tell color just by feel," she said, "so why can't you?"

"Helen Keller is a wonderful lady to whom many supernatural abilities have been attributed," I patiently explained, "but no one can tell color by feel, not even Helen Keller."

"If you really tried, you could learn to feel color just like Helen Keller can," she insisted. "You mean to tell me that you can't feel color at all?" she shouted by now. At this point I was prompted by an irresistible inner impulse. "Well," I answered quietly, "I can feel blue on Monday."

With that, she lost her composure. She sent me to the principal's office with a note declaring that I had been impudent and impertinent. The principal listened carefully as I related the events of that afternoon in my English class. To my surprise, he erupted into a hardy laugh as I came to the end of my tale. He shook my hand, took me around the corner to a vending machine and bought me a bar of chocolate. He instructed me to return to class the following afternoon. Miss Storm conducted the class as if nothing had ever happened. And, I got out of writing a composition.

Peggy Elliott

It's All in How You Look at It

by Peggy Elliott

It's all in how you look at it. A common phrase we usually take to mean something like, "What do you think about the matter?" But in this case, the meaning is intended to be quite literal.

We who are blind have learned that there are indeed many ways to look and that, frequently, things that might seem to be entirely visual may hardly involve the eye at all. Peggy Elliott is Second Vice President of the National Federation of the Blind. Here is what she has to say:

We have a big, hundred-year-old house with lots of wood in it, including big window frames around the 29 windows on the first and second floors. But we hadn't gotten around to curtains beyond sheers for quite a few years. Last year, we bit the bullet.

Both my husband Doug and I are blind. We decided to have an interior decorator named Kathy help us choose window treatments. She came, measured, left, and called us a week or so later to come down and see what she had for suggestions.

Kathy showed us five or six alternatives for the 22 windows we were addressing. All highlighted the beautiful wood which we approved of, but we didn't like most of her choices. Kathy would put the sample book on the counter and describe her idea as we touched the samples with our hands and assessed her words according to the look we were seeking. Most of the samples were patterned or striped, and some had lace or frilly stuff as accents. We listened, touched, and hoped for better choices.

When Kathy got to one of the last choices, we both knew it was the one for our home. It was simple—off-white material with a bright swag for the downstairs living spaces. We picked for the three rooms upstairs as well, staying simple as we went.

I didn't want Kathy to think we were rejecting her choices, so I said after a while that we just like simple stuff. Kathy replied: "Well, if someone walks into your house and says that this looks like Kathy did it, then I've failed. I want to help you express your taste, not to impose mine." I felt better about rejecting other options after that.

The curtains are all installed now. Kathy was so pleased with our choice for the main living spaces that she has photographed the result to show to other customers. It was the right choice for us and for our house.

But my husband got a little carried away. After we did the windows, I started saying that we needed to take a year off, take a breather, not spend any more money while we recovered from the cost of beautifying our home. Doug ignored me completely.

He's always wanted to fulfill my life dream of having a grandfather clock. We were so pleased with the curtains that he went ahead and got me a clock for my birthday. It's beautiful. It's over six feet tall, hand-made of cherry wood with beveled glass insets, and chimes beautifully without being overwhelming.

The very best part is that my clock was made for us by a blind friend.

We know a blind person who loves to make things. When my husband first considered getting the clock (even after I pleaded for financial restraint, I might add), he immediately thought of our blind friend whose work is careful, precise, and always lovely.

Now, when people enter our dining room, they say: "Oooooh." The curtains look as though they've always been there— just right for the house. In between two of the dressed-up windows stands my clock, causing the "Oooooh." All who have seen it want one for themselves.

Ordinary stories? Doesn't everyone decorate and give precious gifts to loved ones? Yes, and blind people do the same thing. We know what we like, have just as good and bad taste as others, and express that taste in the homes we live in.

But Doug and I have the good luck and good sense to belong to the National Federation of the Blind, which has taught us to believe in ourselves, not only in getting jobs, paying bills, and working in our communities but in the other areas of living such as choosing how our home is to look.

Through the Federation, we have learned that we can touch things and listen to descriptions to decide what things look like and then choose the things that express ourselves.

Without the self-confidence gained through our blind friends in the Federation, we might have let Kathy choose, thinking her sight was more important than our taste. But not us!

And who ever heard of going to a blind person for fine craftsmanship? We have. Not every blind person is a fine craftsman, but our friend Mickey is as good a craftsman as anyone I know, blind or sighted.

It all comes down to how you look at it, and we have learned through the Federation to look at ourselves as capable, competent people and to look at other blind people the same way. Choose our own curtains? You bet, and they're in the decorator's book of choices. Go to a blind craftsman for a lovely gift? You bet! And we're the envy of everyone we know.

Suzanne Waters

THE COSTS OF CAMOUFLAGE

By Suzanne Waters

Suzanne Waters is a blind woman who lives in Philadelphia and is an active member of the National Federation of the Blind of Pennsylvania. Her experience tells us that the difference between misery and happiness can often be reduced to just one word: belief. Here is what she says:

The summer after I graduated from high school had been unrelentingly hot. Even the wind, when it did stir, was stifling. It felt as though I had been pacing around my house, sweltering and bored, since the beginning of time. Imagine my glee at hearing the wonderful news that a group of friends from my church were going to the beach. "Of course I'll go," I said with enthusiasm.

Although Lake Michigan was less than an hour's drive away from my home, it was rare that I got a chance to spend the day there. Perhaps now that many of my friends could drive, I speculated (while throwing sunscreen and a towel into a duffel bag) this situation would turn around.

Blind since birth and unaware of many of the techniques which people with little or no vision use to acclimate themselves to unfamiliar places, I could not begin to imagine any other way to enjoy Lake Michigan than by depending on a sighted person with a car to get me there and guide me around.

It was like Heaven to splash in the cool lake, getting into fierce water fights and diving under to grab the ankles or tickle the feet of a friend. We were a boisterous group, liberated from school and with our lives stretching gloriously ahead.

After an hour or so of swimming, I decided I wanted to work on my suntan. Reluctantly, one of my companions left the water and guided me to a warm spot on the sand, immediately returning to the waves. I was alone on the crowded beach.

I don't know how long I lay on my back, half listening to distant music from other people's radios. I was almost asleep when I felt something hard bounce off my bare belly. Seconds later, it happened again. Awake but with my eyes closed, I struggled to figure out the mystery.

"Who's this girl?" came a boy's voice from above me. "She's pretty cute."

"I don't know," said another boy. "Let's wake her up and ask her if she wants to go play video games."

The combination of panic and realization that washed over me made my stomach do a sickening flip-flop. These boys thought I was normal, just a "regular girl" who had fallen asleep in the sun. Like adolescent boys everywhere, they were now engaging in the timeless game of teasing a girl they found interesting and attractive.

At that moment, I knew two things for sure. The first was that my family, who had always told me that I was no worse off than anyone else just because I was blind and that I could do almost anything I set my mind to, had been wrong. The evidence was before me: blind people begging for change in the street, standing in unemployment lines, being the dubious heroes of daredevil action thrillers and horror movies.

Despite my good grades and supportive family, I had a premonition that mine would be a life dogged by disbelief—both mine and society's—about what I could be and do. The second thing I knew was that as soon as I opened my eyes and "blew my cover," the boys would slink away, embarrassed, ashamed, and mute.

I made the decision then that, no matter what they did, I would refuse to open my eyes. Over the ensuing minutes, my inert body was the target of several more small stones, a clump of wet sand, and a cupful of lake water. I willed myself to remain completely still and prayed that they would go away, my ruse intact.

As luck would have it, I was rescued by my gaggle of friends, finally tired from their game of water tag. "Leave her alone," they yelled good-naturedly to the boys. "She's trying to sleep." The boys loped away, in search of more interesting diversions.

I felt immensely relieved that I had made it through the ordeal undiscovered, but also empty and sad at having missed the opportunity to have fun with those boys.

Worst of all, it seemed that I could do nothing to change this reality.

In the fall of the following year, I applied for and was awarded a college scholarship through the National Federation of the Blind of Michigan. Although flattered to have won, I felt decidedly uneasy when I learned that I would have to be present at the NFB's state convention in order to receive the award.

I needed the money, but could I possibly stand to be with all of those blind people, groping around incompetently, for an entire weekend? I comforted myself with the thought that my family would be there as well, and I could escape to the hotel room and watch movies if things got too horrible.

There are rare times in our lives when we go into an experience with a negative expectation and are wonderfully surprised by what we find instead. As soon as I entered the convention hotel, I knew I was among friends and role models. I met blind students, entrepreneurs, computer users, and teachers.

I talked with people who had traveled extensively, spoke many languages, and had children of their own. I observed people who boldly reached out and touched their world, unembarrassed to feel for elevator buttons or otherwise explore their environment. In two days, the walls I had allowed to form around me began to crumble away.

Yes, it was undeniable that blindness is feared and misunderstood by many, and thousands of those who cannot see experience discrimination and prejudice. But I started to realize that I was not a helpless victim, forced by circumstance to lie still while the rest of the world left me behind.

I had numerous living examples before me of men and women who had taken control of their individual and collective destiny as blind people. Perhaps I could, after all, open my eyes, let the world recognize me for the unique and talented person I was, and assume my rightful place in society.

As I write these pages on my talking computer, it is another steamy summer. Sixteen years have rushed by since my experience at the beach. After graduating Phi Beta Kappa from a private, liberal arts college in Michigan, I moved to Philadelphia, where I live to this day.

I no longer pace around my home waiting for someone to rescue me from boredom. Instead, when I have free time from my paid and volunteer work responsibilities, I often call friends and initiate activities and travel plans.

Experience has taught me that I am far more limited by misconceptions about blindness—my own and those of society—

than I am by blindness itself. In retrospect, I realize that, had I opened my eyes and admitted my identity as a person who is blind, those boys might have become my friends, and we could have learned a great deal from each other.

I am no longer willing to pay the cost of camouflage. I would much rather stand proud, my eyes open, ready to create my own opportunities.

Jan Omvig Gawith

GOLF WIDOW OR GOLFER— I HAD TO CHOOSE

by Jan Omvig Gawith

Jan Gawith has been an active member and leader in the National Federation of the Blind for nearly forty years. She lives and works in the state of Idaho. In her story Jan tells us how she learned to replace the words, "I can't" with "How can I?" and of the striking difference that transformation made in her life. Here is what she has to say:

As a girl there were few sports which interested me—I couldn't see very well and did not do well. When schoolmates did throw me the ball, be it softball or basketball, I usually missed it or got hit with it. My glasses were often bent or broken. Also, I was usually the last one chosen for the team.

When I tried miniature golf my play was clumsy and hesitant. When bowling I had considerable difficulty finding my ball and then in walking straight. My success was about the same as in miniature golf. And, my friends seemed to have such fun water skiing but always found excuses to keep me from trying. Eventually it became evident to me that they were afraid for my safety. After all, I didn't see very well.

After high school the next ten years of work, college, and teaching were fraught with great difficulty and many frustrations. My eyesight continued to fail. After promptly losing a job I had worked hard to get, a friend suggested that I contact the center for the blind. I wasn't excited by the idea, but I really had little to lose.

Only later did I realize what a fortunate choice I made. And that is how it happened that nearly ten years out of high school my life really began.

The night I was interviewed about entering the training program, I met the head of the agency. Yes, I said that night. He was still at work at 7:30 in the evening. Who else would that have been but Dr. Kenneth Jernigan?

Yes, I was lucky and blessed because my training took place in Iowa in 1960-61 while he was directing programs for the blind there. We all came to know that late nights and early mornings were not unusual to him but rather the norm.

Dr. Jernigan did not pussyfoot around with "You don't see very well," but flatly told me that I was blind. His very direct approach helped me. If memory serves me correctly I gulped and thought, "O.K., now what?"

Very shortly after that evening visit I began as a student at the orientation and adjustment center. There was no more time to worry about that lost job. I was too busy learning—cane travel, typing, home economics, and Braille, or so I thought. In retrospect or with my 20/20 hindsight, I know I was really learning to live. "I can't" had to be eliminated from my vocabulary and "How can I?" inserted. Some activities which I had formerly considered beyond my capacity, if I had considered them at all, became an accepted way of life.

During my year at the center I gained confidence and freedom. I was also introduced to the National Federation of the Blind, and it has been an important part of my life for more than thirty-five years.

My formal training at the center ended in April of 1961—the learning from the training has never ceased. And, with the exception of about two years, I have either worked and/or been in college ever since. One of the most exciting jobs I have had was serving as secretary to a member of the state legislature.

I believe that just being seen carrying on my normal activities by members of the legislature was helpful. We secretaries were told that we would be dismissed if we lobbied the legislators—simply walking down the halls with my long white cane for the mail probably influenced them. Otherwise, I was careful to only answer their questions. And there were many! My favorite long-term job was working with other blind persons at the Idaho Commission for the Blind.

But what about the water skiing, bowling, and golf? I've done them all! The year before my husband Harry (who is sighted) and I were married we joined a bowling league of which we were members for twenty-three years and still continue to league bowl. I use a rail to help me walk straight.

A few people complain about the rails, but not many, and the only perfect game I have ever witnessed was bowled against us with the rails. We threatened to take them down whenever that fellow was an opponent after that. He refused.

When I was about sixty, my husband took up golf with a vengeance. This presented me with a new dilemma. After all, it is one thing to bowl using a rail and quite another to strike that tiny little ball which is about four feet from your hand. And, after all, I hadn't been able even to do miniature golf when I could see some.

I temporarily forgot the "how can I" aspect of my way of life. I rode around in the golf cart part of the time, but five hours of that gets boring. I can see now that I put some strain on the golfing relatives because my sister-in-law sometimes decided she would rather not go.

One evening a family group was in the yard knocking golf balls around, and my brother-in-law coaxed me to try. They were using whiffle balls which won't go very far. I tried and finally connected with a few, but

I wanted a real ball. Well, the first one that I hit went about twenty feet—behind me!

I finally did hit one that ended up going nearly a block. Also, I knew that there were other blind people who golfed, and I began to think about "how can I" instead of making excuses. I understand that none of us will or cares to do everything—I still don't wish to snow ski or float the river—but simply not to try was rather shameful. As Paul Harvey would say, "And now for the rest of the story."

Yes, I began going golfing some six years ago, and I was really awful going by the scores. I have dropped from thirty to sixty strokes off the game on a given day, and I am still awful as scores go, but, as a friend of mine said of himself, "It only costs me about ten cents a stroke!"

The best part, however, is that instead of staying home all weekend doing such exciting things as laundry, I am often at the city course being highly frustrated along with my husband. The truth about golf is that it frustrates everyone, and I'm not there to be a professional golfer, but to spend some quality time with my husband.

We also take this time to educate others about blindness. Golfers are, for the most part, a great bunch of people. Some openly believe it is amazing that I golf. We spend some time disabusing them of this notion. Others ask questions and volunteer to line me up.

One fellow from Baltimore who was in the group behind us said, "I just knew you would be slow when I saw you (the cane), but now I see it is not you but the guys in front of us who are slowing us all down."

Once I hit a thirty-one yard putt. Another time I missed an eight inch putt. Considering this, with tongue in cheek, I must say my golf game is truly amazing!

I will doubtless never be a particularly good golfer, mostly because I do not physically have the strength to smash the ball, making long distance hits out of the question.

I do have fun, get some much needed exercise, and I'm not a golf widow. The most important thing is that I went back to the "How can I" mode of thinking that I learned so many years ago from my friend and mentor, Dr. Kenneth Jernigan. My thanks go to him for helping me to a quality and fruitful life.

Shawn Mayo

But Mommy Will Be Mad at Me

by Shawn Mayo

Shawn Mayo is president of the National Federation of the Blind's organization of blind college students. Her story explores her mother's conflict between belief and fear and shows that changing what we think about blindness in the deepest levels of our souls isn't easy. Here is what she has to say:

"But, mommy will be mad at me," pleaded Ashley. What! I thought, astonished. All I had asked my 3-year-old sister was whether she wanted to take a walk to my university and then to Hardee's.

When my mother went back to work, I had told her that I could arrange my schedule to allow me to watch my youngest sister, Ashley, once a week. What a wonderful opportunity it would be for me to spend quality time with my sister and take a break from the demands of school and daily routine. I enjoy working with children; in fact, I am pursuing a career as a psycho-oncologist, working with children and adolescents with cancer.

Most of the time when I watch Ashley, my mother brings her over to my apartment in the morning and picks her up in the early evening. Ashley keeps me going constantly. She is a very intelligent and curious child whose attention span is that of a typical 3-year-old—short!

Sometimes we play with Play-Doh, creating different animals and various objects that Ashley thinks up. The imagination of a child is priceless. What appears to be a lump of clay with indentations and another chunk of attached clay is at times a horse—which in the next breath can be a tree. We also play a lot on the computer. She loves to hear my computer "talk" with the speech synthesizer.

"Let's go to Disney dot com," is an all-too-familiar request. My computer with speech has provided a useful tool for me to work with her on the alphabet and the sounds of letters. Sometimes we bake cookies, and other times I read her a story in Braille.

Having her here has given me the opportunity to teach her about blindness. She is learning at an early age that blind people can do the same things as sighted people but that sometimes we do these things in a different way.

One day when Ashley came over she kept talking about how my sister Genesis took her to see a movie and then to McDonald's. I did not want Ashley to think that we could not go to places outside my apartment and yard. So, I decided it would be fun to take her to my university to see the fountain outside the library and then walk to Hardee's, where she could get a happy meal.

"Do you want to see where I go to school and then get a happy meal from Hardee's?" I asked Ashley.

"Yes!" Ashley exclaimed. I proceeded to put her shoes and coat on. Then I grabbed my cane. We asked my roommate, Sheila, who is also blind, if she wanted to come along and, soon the three of us headed outside. When we got outside, I asked Ashley, "Are you ready?"

"But, Mommy will be mad at me," she pleaded.

What! I thought, astonished. All I had asked my 3 year-old-sister was if she wanted to take a walk to my university and then to Hardee's.

"What do you mean, Mommy will be mad at you?" I asked Ashley.

"Mommy said we can't go by the street," Ashley responded.

At first I was hurt and could not believe that my own mother, who had always encouraged me to go after my dreams, who knew about my travels across the country, who had driven me to the National Federation of the Blind's training center in Minneapolis to learn alternative techniques of blindness (including mobility) had told my little sister such a thing! But, she had.

It was one thing for me to control my own life, but my mother could not bring herself to believe that a blind person could care for a child away from the "safety" of one's own home.

I knew my sister trusted me. I also knew that, for the most part, she did what our mother told her to do. But, I could not let her grow up with the misconception that her sister could not take her anywhere because she was blind. So, I decided to talk to her about the ways that I do the same things that other people do.

"How do blind people read?" I asked.

"Braille," she immediately responded as if I should know that.

"You're right. How do Sheila and I use the computer?" I went on.

"The letters and the mouse," she replied.

"Yes, that's true." (I had to remember I was talking to a 3-year-old.) "And, it talks to me, too. What is this?" I inquired while pointing to my cane.

"Your cane, Sissy," she answered.

Of course, she knew it was my cane. Ashley loves to go and get my cane for me whenever we go to the laundry room, check the mail, or play outside. Often she will grab my collapsible cane for herself and mimic my using my cane.

We talked about the cane and how I use it as a tool to find the curb to know where the streets are, and how I use my ears to hear where the cars are. It is amazing how quickly children can be open to learning and replacing their misconceptions.

So, off we went on our adventure. The grass on the sides of the sidewalk became water, ridden with alligators! On our way we paused to watch a squirrel that Ashley had spotted. Bright kid, I thought as Ashley told me how she learned at the Nature Center that a squirrel uses its tail to protect it from the hot sun and wet rain.

We examined pine cones and listened to the birds as we walked hand in hand to the university. I showed Ashley where some of my classes were, and we headed over to sit by the fountain. After splashing in the water some we decided to go get lunch. Then, off on another adventure, we went to find the rewards that fast food had to offer.

That evening when my mother came to pick Ashley up, Ashley was excitedly relaying all the fun things that she had done that day. I asked my mother why she had told Ashley that she could not go on walks with me.

"It's dangerous," was all my mother would say.

It's because I'm blind I told her. And, even though she denied it, we both knew that that was the underlying reasoning behind her belief. Mom had thought that because I am blind, I would not be able to keep Ashley safe.

As I thought about it, I understood my mother's worry. Like all of us (blind and sighted alike) she has absorbed society's beliefs about blindness. At one level mother knew that (because of the very training she herself helped me to get) the chances of Ashley's getting hurt while in my care were really not greater than if I were sighted. But, she was still afraid.

It will take time for all of us to come to a different understanding of blindness.

"Let's go for a walk, Sissy," Ashley often says. Perhaps we have to grow up with it.

Noel Nightingale

BEHOLD BEAUTY

by Noel Nightingale

Noel Nightingale is President of the National Federation of the Blind of Washington State and a member of our National Board of Directors. She is a mother, a wife, an attorney. Here she reflects on the nature of beauty and the magical moments of life:

My husband, Jim Peterson, and I recently had the joy of having a baby. Her name is Leila Nightingale Peterson. She weighed 6 pounds, 3 ounces at birth and is now a couple of months old. Objectively speaking, Leila is absolutely perfect. She is smart, advanced for her age and is extremely well-behaved, crying only when it is convenient for us. And, she is beautiful.

One of my nurses told me the day we left the hospital, "All the nurses are talking about how beautiful your baby is: one of the prettiest they've seen." Earlier, my nurse asked her colleagues whether they had told me what they thought. They said they had not because the mother was blind and they did not want to make her feel bad.

She admonished them that all mothers want to hear that their babies are beautiful. I thanked my nurse for telling me and told her that I already knew that Leila is lovely but was glad to hear that others thought so too. This exchange reminded me that I had once wondered whether beauty would be denied to me as a blind person.

I will never forget the only time I saw a butterfly up close. It was when I could still see. I was with a friend on the top of a mountain in the Blue Mountains of southeastern Washington. We were having a picnic, with all of the usual picnic supplies. Among other things, we had a carton of orange juice with us. At one point, the butterfly landed on the orange juice carton.

I slowly moved my head closer and closer to the butterfly. Amazingly enough, it did not fly away. My face was just inches away from the butterfly, and I could see all the details of its coloring—yellow, white, and black. I could see the lines where each color ended and the next began. I could see the delicate edges of the wings. It was a magical moment.

At this point in my life, I had recently been diagnosed with a degenerative eye disorder and knew I would soon be blind. I savored the moment of seeing the intricate detail of this handsome creature. I worried that when I became blind I would never again experience the beauty found in such rare and privileged moments.

A few years ago, I was riding in a car with Jim and noticed that I could not tell what color the sky was. I knew that it was blue, but I could not see that it was. It looked like it could be either green or purple or blue but did not look definitely like any of those colors. I cried because I did not want to lose the ability to enjoy those moments when we pause and savor the beauty that can be found in our world.

For many years now, I have been unable to see color or detail. The visual world is a blur of neutral, undefined objects and people. Despite this loss, I have continued to live a normal life and appreciate beauty. I have married, had Leila, work, am a member of several boards of directors of nonprofit organizations, and occasionally find time to travel.

Some time after I had gone blind, Jim and I took a trip to Europe with our tandem bicycle. We rode from London, England, to Madrid, Spain. We spent several weeks riding in the Pyrenees Mountains of Spain.

During one stretch, we found ourselves low on food and out of water. We had underestimated the number of miles between towns and had no hope of finding water for an entire day. We were riding in the searing sun of the Spanish summer. To make matters worse, we were riding up mountains most of the day. I began to cry because I was thirsty and afraid. There were no cars, no homes, and no hope that we would be rescued from our thirst and hunger. We continued riding, though, because there was nothing else to do.

After hours of riding in this desperate state, we rounded a bend in the road and heard water running. A pipe was sticking out of the side of a small hill, and water was pouring out of it! Not only that, but there was a sign next to it that said, "Potable Water" (in Spanish). It was absolutely magical. In the middle of nowhere in those dry mountains, was cold, drinkable water. We stopped, put our heads under the spout, gulped the water, and rejoiced.

There are two middle-aged brothers living in Louisiana who have been blind since their birth. When they were born, their parents did not know that their blind babies could grow up, have careers, marry, raise families and be active members of their communities. Their parents had such low expectations for them that they placed their blind boys, who were only a couple of years apart in age, in a room with cement floors and left them there.

They fed them, but they did not teach them how to use the bathroom. They did not read to them, send them to school or play with them. The two boys had such little intellectual or social stimulation that they became mentally retarded. After their parents died, they were sent to a residential institution for retarded people.

One day, the brothers' case worker gave each one an orange. It became apparent that they had never before touched or eaten an orange. They held their oranges, smelled them, marveled at the oranges' coolness, shape, texture and sweet aroma.

Beauty *is* experienced by blind people. Both the Louisiana brothers and I, as blind people, have experienced the depths of the world's beauty. While our experiences are not visual, they have been as profound as if we were seeing the wings of a butterfly or eating an orange for the first time.

Although we share blindness, the difference between the Louisiana brothers' experience with blindness and my experience fifty years later is marked. I have had a range of opportunities available to me that was denied to the brothers.

What has happened between the time the Louisiana brothers were children and when I became blind? The National Federation of the Blind has worked to let people know that blindness does not prevent people from living normal lives.

Were the brothers born today, members of the National Federation of the Blind could have told the brothers' parents the truth: blindness need not be a tragedy if blind people are given proper training in the use of a long white cane, taught to read Braille, allowed to use special computer equipment, and develop other skills.

Not only does blindness not have to be a tragedy, but we can enjoy even those fleeting, magical moments that make life the wonderful gift that it is.

DOING WHAT'S NECESSARY

by Stephen O. Benson

Sighted people are often curious about the simple modifications that blind people make in order to get on with ordinary life. Mostly they are not ingenious or complex. The simpler the better is a good rule to follow, and blind youngsters are particularly clever at applying the principle to their play.

Steve Benson, President of the NFB of Illinois and Member of the NFB Board of Directors, has struck up a friendship with one of his fellow commuters into downtown Chicago. The woman recently expressed eagerness to know how Steve has developed the little tricks that he uses every day.

Steve began thinking back to childhood and the modifications he and his friends made that enabled him to join in neighborhood games. The following article was the result. Here it is:

The Hawthorn was a fine old gray-stone, twelve-flat building in Chicago's Lincoln Park area across the street from De Paul University. It boasted polished, dark hardwood millwork; oak parquet floors; and formal marble entrances. Sometime in the 1920's it was converted to a fifty-nine-unit rooming house. It was there that my mother and I settled in 1943; I was just a year and a half old.

Two significant things occurred at about that time: doctors at Children's Memorial Hospital determined that I had retinitis pigmentosa, and my mother became manager of the Hawthorn. Since we lived where my mother worked, she was able to guide and mold her young son in ways she could not have otherwise. The Hawthorn and its inhabitants had much to do with who I have become.

When I entered first grade, I was unable to read standard print. So school officials placed me in what were then called "sight-saving" classes. I could not identify facial features. I could not follow the flight of a batted or thrown ball. I could not see a bird in a tree. I had no idea what blindness was.

At some point the notion of blindness was raised, but I did not regard myself as blind, for I could see. Somewhere along the line it was suggested that I was "half-blind," and that seemed okay.

As I moved from second to third to fourth grade, my visual acuity diminished while the print I was expected to read became smaller. Reading became more and more difficult. I have very distinct memories of sitting at my desk, staring out the window, trying to puzzle out the print figures on the page in front of me. It was like reading gray print on gray paper.

My teacher printed my math problems in large figures in India ink, and still I struggled. That was the middle of fourth grade, and it was another year before I was

Steve Benson

transferred to a school where I could learn to read and write Braille.

The prevailing theory then was that vision should be used until it was absolutely necessary to learn Braille. That theory was based on age-old misconceptions about blindness, and to a disturbing degree that misguided theory persists today. Inevitably those beliefs colored my attitude toward my loss of vision.

For all practical purposes my formal education began when I reached the second half of fifth grade. Until that time I had never read a book from the library; I couldn't. I began learning Braille in September of 1952. By January of 1953 I was able to read a biography of Andrew Jackson. It was not easy. Many of the bad reading habits I had developed as I tried to read print carried over to Braille. In fact, some of those bad reading habits stayed with me well into adulthood.

Although school work was difficult for me, I mastered a variety of other skills at home with enthusiasm. Nick and I met in the back yard of the Hawthorn when we were about three years old. Both of us lived in single-parent households with no siblings, so we bonded like brothers. Though I was legally blind, neither of us had any idea that my limited vision should make a difference.

Nick and I learned what my sight would and would not allow me to do. We invented alternative techniques or devices that enabled me to participate in virtually every childhood activity. Nobody instructed us in the design of devices or techniques; we just did what had to be done.

The Hawthorn was loaded with kids. The back yard was thirty feet wide and about a hundred feet long, all cement. It was like a Hollywood stage set, ever changing. One day railroad tracks were drawn with chalk, complete with switches and crossovers. Our wagons and tricycles traversed the cross-country paths until it rained or until we tired of it; then the yard became something else: a baseball diamond, a football gridiron, a site for statue maker or red light/green light, and more. I participated in all of these activities. We organized teams and devised alternative ways for me to play ball. I was fully involved.

At about the time Nick and I were ten, we met Tom, who lived in the building next door. Nick, Tom, and I joined other kids in the neighborhood in softball, touch football, basketball, and track events. In each of these sports the alternatives we developed worked for me and for the rest of the kids.

In softball (using the sixteen-inch ball that is common to the Chicago area), I was usually the pitcher. The catcher would position himself behind home plate, clap his hands, and receive my deliveries. When the pitches were too far out of the strike zone, he would tell me the location so that I could make a correction. My objective was to hit the corners so that the batter would be less likely to drive the ball up the middle since I could not field a line drive in the conventional manner. I also tried to keep the ball low so the batter would hit the ball into the ground.

Batting presented a different set of challenges. I could not hit a pitched ball with any consistency, so I balanced the ball on the finger tips of my left hand and swung the bat with my right. I became surprisingly skilled at hitting the ball, and I had the advantage of being able to place my hits pretty accurately. But I must admit that I did strike myself out on occasion, to almost everybody's delight. It was always challenging, and we had great fun.

The alternatives we devised for softball were typical of what we did for all sports. The modifications were really minimal. I played; I prevailed; I experienced ignominious defeat; but I competed and am richer for having done so.

Nick and Tom were extraordinary guys. They were imaginative, patient, and willing to learn along with me. I guess the only thing they eventually balked at was allowing me to work on their cars. They were adamant that they didn't want me to hurt my hands. I was never able to persuade them to change their minds. I suppose that by then we had begun to accumulate the caution of adulthood.

Arts and crafts were a way of life for my mother. She got me involved in puppetry when I was about six. By the time I was nine years old, I was performing before audiences of up to 300. Later I performed as a part-time professional puppeteer for seventeen years and was a charter member of the Chicagoland Puppetry Guild. Mother organized talent shows in which the kids in the building and the surrounding neighborhood participated. We kids were involved in every aspect of the productions, from printing and selling tickets to painting sets to setting up a hundred or so chairs for the audience. I remember thinking about the shows that this was not fun, but in retrospect those performances had tremendous value for all of us, especially for a blind kid. We learned something about teamwork and collective effort.

When I was about seven years old, my mother began to require me to do certain chores around the Hawthorn. I installed rolls of toilet paper, carried messages to the tenants, and counted linen and towels. As I grew older and taller, I changed light bulbs, took telephone messages which I typed, shoveled snow, and cleaned the yard and basement.

By the time I was twelve or thirteen, I collected rent, recorded payment, and issued receipts. When I was sixteen, the building's owner paid me the staggering sum of $50 a month for my toil. It was my first paying job.

At nine years of age several of my friends and I joined a local Cub Scout pack. I was expected to participate in all of the pack projects, including weaving a reed basket and making plaster casts of animal heads. My lion's head turned out to be an astonishing shade of purple.

At eleven I joined Boy Scout Troop 300. All the boys and the scoutmaster were blind. That was my first contact with a blind adult. We were expected to fulfill all of the requirements for promotion; there were no exceptions. We made a crystal set radio and a one-tube radio, and they had to work. We erected tents and cooked on fires we had to build. We learned to swim, and we competed in aquatic events at Boy Scout camp. Scouting, puppetry, and the back-yard talent shows helped me build confidence.

My mother taught me how to use the public transit system in Chicago. She understood the necessity for a blind person to master its use, so I learned which busses and trains went where.

During the summer of 1956 I began learning to travel independently with a forty-six-inch white cane. My travel teacher was blind. As a high school freshman I was required to get to and from school on public transportation. Mastery of independent travel skills and good judgment were essential. These skills have enabled me to travel confidently to thirty-four states for business and pleasure.

As I reflect on my childhood, it is difficult for me to imagine that I missed much. Had it not been for my extraordinarily talented mother, who had the sense to let me grow and learn, and had it not been for Nick and Tom, who were not for the most part afraid of blindness, growing up would surely have been different. Nick, Tom, and I are still friends. Our lives bear the scars of experience, but we often recall the many events of childhood that inspire a smile, a chuckle, or a back-slapping laugh.

You can help us spread the word...

...about our Braille Readers Are Leaders contest for blind schoolchildren, a project which encourages blind children to achieve literacy through Braille.

...about our scholarships for deserving blind college students.

...about Job Opportunities for the Blind, a program that matches capable blind people with employers who need their skills.

...about where to turn for accurate information about blindness and the abilities of the blind.

Most importantly, you can help us by sharing what you've learned about blindness in these pages with your family and friends. If you know anyone who needs assistance with the problems of blindness, please write:

Marc Maurer, President
National Federation of the Blind
1800 Johnson Street, Suite 300
Baltimore, Maryland 21230-4998

Other Ways You Can Help the National Federation of the Blind

Write to us for tax-saving information on bequests and planned giving programs.

OR

Include the following language in your will:

"I give, devise, and bequeath unto National Federation of the Blind, 1800 Johnson Street, Suite 300, Baltimore, Maryland 21230, a District of Columbia nonprofit corporation, the sum of \$_____ (or "___ percent of my net estate" or "The following stocks and bonds:_____") to be used for its worthy purposes on behalf of blind persons."

Your Contributions Are Tax-deductible